I0223621

SOMEHOW,
I HAVEN'T DROWNED

A Collection of Poems

by

Robin Gabbert

BLUE LIGHT PRESS ◆ 1ST WORLD PUBLISHING

1ˢᵗ WORLD
PUBLISHING

SAN FRANCISCO ◆ FAIRFIELD ◆ DELHI

Winner of the Fran Claggett-Holland Award for Poetry

Somehow, I Haven't Drowned

Copyright ©2025 by Robin Gabbert

All rights reserved. Printed in the United States of America. No part of this book may be used or reproduced in any manner whatsoever without written permission except in the case of brief quotations embodied in critical articles and reviews. For information contact:

1st World Library
PO Box 2211
Fairfield, IA 52556
www.1stworldpublishing.com

Blue Light Press
www.bluelightpress.com
bluelightpress@aol.com

Book & Cover Design
Melanie Gendron
melaniegendron999@gmail.com

Cover Art
"Noah's Ark" by Melanie Gendron

Author Photo
Sari Singerman

First Edition

Library of Congress Cataloging-in-Publication Data

ISBN: 978-1-4218-3591-4

*"Poetry is thoughts that breathe,
and words that burn."*

– Thomas Gray

Dedications

This book has been in the works for five years, at least since my book *Diary of a Mad Poet* was published. I've had help from many poets and mentors along the way including the amazing Fran Claggett-Holland, Les Bernstein, my sisters in the Blue Moon Poetry Salon, Diane Frank of Blue Light Press, who guided me through numerous workshops, and my cohorts at the PEP collective (you know who you are). My husband Con who cooks our dinners and son Willem have been a daily support to me, along with my sister Terri Collins, close friends and sounding boards Barbara Abbott, Karen Fitzgerald, Bridget Hayes and Lisha Adela Garcia. I offer profuse thanks to all these generous people. Poetry can be lonely work. It helps when you have smart and funny friends.

Foreward

by Fran Claggett-Holland

"*Somehow, I Haven't Drowned.*" Don't overlook the title of this amazing collection of poems by Robin Gabbert. Robin, like Robert Frost, is a trickster poet – with subtler meaning always present in her poems. It is easy to get swept up in her ability to get right to the heart of one tragedy after another, but don't forget to notice that she emerges strong and determined in the next poem. She has an uncanny ability to take her readers to the depth, while always magically letting them know that she operates at both a much higher and deeper level.

The book is beautifully structured, so take a minute to follow her clues from "Taking the Plunge," through the "Whirlpool," through ocean-oriented sections to, eventually, "Treading Water." She is masterful in building mood and tone in all parts of the book, and awakening in her readers almost a companionship, before returning us to her vivid finales.

Keep an eye out for this author's work. She is also prolific in the realm of ekphrastic poetry and her writing will surprise you when you are least expecting it.

Fran Claggett-Holland is a teacher, poet, and dog-lover who loves to see others' poetry dreams materialize. At ninety-five she still leads a weekly poetry group on Zoom and gives a monthly "Deep Reading" class focusing on one important poet. She has edited at least eight poetry anthologies and authored six books of poetry. Her most recent solo book of poems, *Under the Wings of the Crow*, includes new poems, and poems selected from previous collections – *Black Birds and Other Birds* (Taurean Horn Press), *Crow Crossings*, and *The Consciousness of Stone* (both RiskPress) and *Moments with Madge: Lux Aeterna* (the White Crow Press).

Table of Contents

1. Take the Plunge 1

Invisible 3
Kisses 5
Baby Girl of My Heart 7
Letter to Someone Long Left Behind 9
Bloodlines 10
Reckoning 11
Childbirth, Rural Ohio 1955 12
Pa-Paw 13
Posthumus Epithalamion for Ethel and Sid 14

2. Whirlpool 17

Thunder 19
Storms 20
The Dead Moth 21
The Things That Haunt Me 22
I Never Took a Razor to My Wrists 24

3. The Ocean is Deep 26

Even Sea Serpents 29
Splitting Hairs 30
On the Edge 31
It's Happening Again 32
Tangled 33
We Gather at the Altar 34
Vincent, Are the Trees in St. Remy Truly so Frightening 35
A Parting 36
Master of Dark Looks 37
Between Wolves and Stars 38
When They're Too Young to Tell You Where It Hurts 40

Revisiting a Loved One Lost 41
Diminishing 43

4. Letting the Waves Wash Over Me 45

Snapshots From a Dream 47
Now You See Him, Now You Don't 48
Verklempt 49
Blank Page Syndrome (BPS) 50
The Poetry Tree 51
Puppy Love 53
Willem 54
Lemonade Dreams 56

5. Treading Water 57

Mating Games 59
Glitter 61
Road Tripping 62
Doors with No Numbers 63
Nose Job 64
White Buffalo 65
A Letter to Franz Kafka 66
War 69
Dental Hygiene 70
Crow Wisdom 72
Death Throes 73
Morphine Dreams 78

Acknowledgements 80

About the Author 83

1.

TAKE THE PLUNGE

Invisible

after Rita Dove's Daystar

I find my palace
among ordinary things,
    amidst stars and trees.

Slip into that space
between dark and light —
find a niche,
    enter my palace,
    which is not a palace.

I am not a prisoner here,
but at this moment
leaving is unfathomable.

No need to return
to the creature who snaps
and growls, finds ways
    to turn simple things
    into squabbles.

I'll stay here —
write him a poem,
paint him into a mural,
pick up his pieces
    and sew them like animal hides
    until they make a pleasing form.

Eventually, I will go back,
    back to see ones I love.
    They are why I stayed,
    stayed for decades —

even after the meat
        started to spoil,
the dessert
no longer appealing.

Now

        I am primeval.
        And can always
visit my palace –
the soothing fog
between the dimness
and the dusk

        as there are those
who do not notice:
the shift in the air,
the brief flicker of leaves,
the glaze of eyes,
a distant stare, or

the too long
sharpening
of knives.

Kisses

Fifteen, the year I learned
what it really was to kiss.
Oh, I had kissed before

made out in cars, on couches
tried on the experience
with boys going through
the same kissing motions –
lips together or mouths wide open
with flopping tongues, like eels
on an exploratory mission.

But at fifteen, a boy with freckles
and a mischievous smile
touched me
with his tentative, unhurried,
soft seeking lips and
gentle tongue.

The universe drifted
in a slow-moving arc
around us. Eyes closed,
I could feel only
the pinprick of
stars down my spine,
could not see them
spinning around us.

I was spun into raw silk,
immersed into a warm cocoon,
as we stood beside
my porchlight each night

hoping, it would not be
the last time
that a kiss
could make my bones
light up
like luminarias.

Baby Girl of my Heart

I had such plans for you,
things we would do together –
read *Good Night Moon,*
sing with Art Garfunkel
and waltz around the room,
cuddle on the couch.

"Baby girl of my heart"
that's how I think of you.
Even though you were never born.
Even though I can't know
if you would have been a boy or a girl.
I like to think of you as my first daughter,
the one I still carry in my heart.

Even if you fell from my womb,
were washed away in blood
caught on cotton panties I couldn't
bear to keep, couldn't bear
to throw away (for years).

Then at the hospital, so sterile.
Doctor's words spoken but barely heard.
I watched his fleshy mouth move
like a fish out of water. I wanted out –
to be away from him
away – from the lights, the linoleum.
I wanted to tell him no, no.
You're still with me.

They say the heart has four
chambers, but I say it has five.

Because you're here, in that small
chamber I made for you
with soft blankets and a tiny dog
to keep you company.

Even these decades later
I sometimes hear you
murmur, as I lay still,
curled in on myself.

Letter to Someone Long Left Behind

I have scarcely thought of you these last few years
since I moved from Alaska, where we met, decades ago.

I rarely saw you, even during my last years living there,
and I admit I had moved on, married, had children, a dog.

I wondered why you didn't. You lived with different women
but never made it official, became the dad you could have been.

Did you ever, like me, wonder how stars get crossed?
And what one must do to untangle them?

Are they like gnarled jump ropes or
spider webs that need unweaving?

Do you too…too often focus on those few moments
when a pivot was possible. When one of us might not

have been afraid to offend the status quo
not afraid to speak our minds, our hearts?

Bloodlines

after the poem Genealogy by Betsy Sholl

One parent was a dark suit, the other an emerald sheath.
One was Coke bottle lenses, the other – Waterford crystal.

Till late at night, the girl would see the light on in the den.
On the other side of the house, hear only sighs.

One parent was a red T-bird convertible, the other a Pixie haircut
before Mia made it fashionable.

The tattoo on her back was a whirlpool.

One parent was a mirage, the other too close to see without
        distortion.
One an enigma, the other Good Housekeeping guaranteed.

One of her parents she read voraciously, the other she only
        skimmed.
One was a hunter, the other a nester.

In the revolving door of her becoming,
one kept raising the bar, the other kept tightening the safety net.
Thus, her troubled youth, unexpected early exodus.

Still, trying to be the best of both, she kept skinning her knees –
a girl swimming upstream, looking for purchase.

Reckoning

based on Charlotte Salomon's Painting
"Dreaming of a Life in Heaven"

Mother, you lie in your red-quilted bed
love in your eyes as you look at me, touch me.
As I leave, I do not notice your weak caress
or the hovering Angels that wait outside
to tally your sins, count your acts of kindness.
They stand at their prismed window like tellers
at a bank or ticket takers at the bus depot.
That came to me later in a dream.

I was not there
when your soul rose
to heaven in slices,
your life parsed
into slivers rising.
At first, I wanted to rejoice.
A crowd awaited your arrival.
Some whispered, reproachful.
But there you stood.

Then I woke,
soaked in a cold sweat
recalling God –
perched at the entrance,
was not smiling
and had one hand
concealed behind his back.

Childbirth, 1950s Rural Ohio

The seed was planted three times
and three times lost. Once, it had doubled.
Finally, she survived the early months
without the bleeding, the wrenching sorrow.
Every day that passed without blood,
was a small miracle, more reason to take care
and to be afraid.
When the labor pains finally came,
it was still too soon by two months.
Despite her small body's attempts to expel me,
even when her efforts were successful
with no anesthesia, she continued to suffer.
The sheath of skin that swaddled me
had grown fast to her womb,
was not leaving, without a struggle.
Possessed by an afterbirth that refused to detach,
attended by an old-world doctor
who thought the ancient ways best,
we lay in a country hospital
separate beds – apart yet together.
Our eardrums become
etched with her screams.
Decades later
the screams remain,
engraved, embedded.
Remembering, writing,
cannot erase
the sound
of her suffering.

Pa-Paw

When Pa-Paw was young
he looked like Sean Connery
dark hair slicked back and
a smile that said, *I'm all that
and whipped cream on top.*

A few decades later
he was rail thin, shoulders hunched,
wrist bones sticking out of his cuffs,
no hair to speak of.
We grandkids tiptoed around him.

He teased my little sister
after she found a sparkling black rock,
just sure it was black gold.
He told her, "No, that's a pig turd."
and he laughed and laughed.
She held her ground, mumbling
"NO, it's black gold...."
Then he went to stoke the fire
at the big rusty oil drum where
he burned the trash every day.

He died when I was eleven.
I was sobbing after the funeral.
My Mom felt so touched.
But I was sad we had
missed the school play.
I had a lead role and
the funeral had taken all day.

Posthumous Epithalamion for Ethel and Sid

Ethel, daughter of a blind Irishwoman,
wide saucer eyes bluer than her hair was black –
she was shy smile and pearls in the faded Daguerreo
but she clipped off the extra thumb
of a new-born baby
as a nurse trained by old Doc.

Sid broke his arm delivering messages
by motorcycle in World War I, then was
a brakeman on the B&O.
He rode the rails for days
before returning for doses
of her generous laugh, chicken-and-dumplings,
and nights together on the porch.

The wooden swing creaked
till the children were asleep.
Then, following fireflies
in the stairway windows,
he'd lead her upstairs quietly. She,
still prone to giggle like a schoolgirl.

Seventh daughter of a seventh daughter,
Ethel had visions, prescient dreams,
and sometimes knew my undisclosed
nightmares, location of lost keys,
things still to occur.

Sid later turned gruff
as the TB ate his lungs –
afraid to share a sip of coffee
with a five-year-old me.

But he'd still smile and untie her apron
when she was least expecting it.

Now, the porch swing
of the old house
on Gallia Street   is gone.
It's someone else's house now,
run to ruin, left to the ghosts.

But Ethel's blue eyes shine on
in grand-, great-, and great-great grandkids,
and her laugh still infects all
who will remember

Sometimes,
her whispers
still give us chills.

2.
WHIRLPOOL

Warning: Some of the poems in this section involve images of violence or abuse which may be triggering for some.

Thunder

It thunders like an angry stepfather
when mother is out and you're hiding
under the bed, your knees clattering,
your sister in the closet teeth chattering
while old Jackson whimpers in his bed.
It thunders like the crowd cheering a
corrupt politician knowing
he's fondled the fourteen-year-old
volunteer in his van. It thunders like a cat
backed into a corner, a circus clown
who snarls behind the smile.
Like a head-on collision. It thunders
like the slap to your face the first time
you told him no, the first time the dog peed
in the house, the first time he stubbed
his toe and had no one else to blame.
Like your stepfather's prayer asking
for forgiveness saying
he knew not what he did.

Storms

I've always loved rainstorms.
In Florida growing up
they could be quick –
drench you one minute,
sunshine the next,
sidewalks dry again.

If I knew a thunderstorm was coming,
I would sit on the veranda, watch
the black thunderhead threaten
roll toward me like an angry step-father
shades of darkness temporarily hiding
violent flashes then – strikes
that went deep splitting saplings,
reflected by the river
to then seemingly
disappear

but I was safe on the
veranda. Mother always there
with a sweater when the temp
dropped, rocking in the next chair.

Where did you go at night Mama
when the real storms came?

The Dead Moth

We were at Granny's after a trip to the beach – a rare occurrence. So rare, we stayed too long in the sun. In 1966, there was no sunscreen, only iodine with baby oil or Coppertone with no SPF. My tender eleven-year-old back was now a fiery field of blisters. I lay in cool, almost cold water in the mint green porcelain tub staring up at the ceiling lamp where a dead moth lay. A red rubber hot water bottle hung from the towel rack over the tub, dripping.

I knew I should step out onto the green chenille rug, dry off. But before my foot hit the floor and I could get a towel around me, he barged into the bathroom with no lock, no knock, stating some lotion would help my sunburn. I doubted it, but in no position to argue, I stood still while my back was squirted and rubbed with something stinging my open blisters like a hundred wasps. "Isn't that better," he said? Sobbing, I reached for the towel while he twisted me around, started kissing me; his fat rat of a tongue going into my throat. *I'm going to choke*. Grabbing the towel harder, I ran naked with it into the hall.

People say, "Oh, to be a fly on the wall." But I'd rather be the moth in the lamp, come back to life. Flickering with the knowledge of now, I'd bust out of my glass prison, buzz into the eye of the offender, distract – so that young me could more quickly make her escape. Later that night, I would fly into their room, crawl over his greasy head and into his ear canal. I'd make myself small, burrow my body, wrap my lunar legs around tiny hairs until enmeshed, holding fast until death takes both moth and man.

The Things that Haunt Me

are not ethereal
not supernatural

they shimmy not only
at the foot of my bed

under my covers
behind my wallpaper

they're under my fingernails
my skin
and no amount of clipping
stripping or cutting
will destroy them

I have tried repeatedly
to exorcise them
reveal them
call them out

But I know
what really haunts me
is in my mind
memories
of their misdeeds

Yet I continue to make
the past into a bitter pâté
spread it out for poetry
over toast and tea
let it poison the present

then at night I'm back ripping
off the wallpaper
like an bandage
exposing ghastly faces
to the light over
and over and over
again

I Never Took a Razor to My Wrists

my scars are deeper
small   repeating
made by my mind
sharpening the insults
replaying the hurt
while my head shook
back and forth
back and forth
in disbelief

I was only thirteen
how could he side
with her
I'm his own
flesh and blood

Sometimes I wished
I was in an asylum
where I could just read
write be alone

Instead, they took
her away
I'm sure I
got the blame
even though it was me
who rocked her two-year-old
after he spilt his milk
She ran screaming
hands over head
to their bedroom

Obsessively neat
ashes didn't remain
in ashtrays or
crumbs on the table
She even avoided
vacations with
the kids – too messy

but then she came home
from "the hospital"
I had to go

3.
THE OCEAN IS DEEP

Even Sea Serpents

You wash over me
like falling water –
cleansing,
massaging, cooling me
when I run hot,
warming me
when I am cold,
lonely.

You smooth my scales,
nip away at the rough edges.
My claws still need trimming –
but I've used them for so long,
my protection
their surrender comes less easily.

They've caused a few scars
in return for wounds rendered,
but only the deep ones
and never just
for the insults.

But still,
I long for a sure and kind hand
an occasional back rub.

Not many know
sea serpents
like that.

Splitting Hairs

They say she keeps her feelings bottled up.
Yes, I am a classic introvert, I suppose.

However, it might be more
accurate to say:

Her feelings are like
the hand grenade

your crazy Uncle Joe
brought back from 'Nam

and keeps in a shoebox
under the bed

or

like the ball of twine
Muffy bats around the room,

after being dashed back
and forth a few times.

Except when
they're like

hot caramel
on top of an ice cream sundae

or

the face
of a Dali clock.

On the Edge

at the precipice
pebbles collapse
toes curl
small stones slip

I wish I were a fiddler
some other small crab
able to slide into
the lacey recesses
of round-rimmed tafone

listen to the waves
crash below me while
wind in the sea grass plays
a soothing song

until the sunset
colors the sky
and sea-ravens
shoot through the night
on ebony wings

connect continents
dance with the stars
graze constellations
with their grace

me earthbound
wanting nothing more
than to join them

fly
among
the Pleiades

It's Happening Again

A Fire Survivor's Lament

yellow gray skies
again
pervade my world

they are the color of the fangs
I want to bare and snap and snarl
at everyone and everything

gray ash falls from the sky
as if snow   was always
the color of sorrow

as if trees   wished
to be licked by flames
before peeling, disintegrating
into fire's embrace

this is the afterbirth
of a fire whose breath lingers
on your clothes and in your hair

and builds a nest in your lungs
like a starling
making
your every breath
rattle
through the branches

Tangled

Our bed, the sheets gnarled, limbs akimbo
still awash in the gold blush of passion.

As always, I turn away from you eventually
hug my cover close, fear losing the closeness

of being encompassed by your shine,
shrouded in the fatal familiarity of your arms/legs

but there's also the fear of being unable to breath,
unable to escape

the confines
of such ecstatic chains.

We Gather at the Altar

imbibe the sacrificial wine
after all   the church is empty
closed for repairs

vandals desecrated a sacred
tapestry slashed through
the eyes the heart of angels

scaffolds interrupt stories
rendered on stained glass
Saints now wander into black holes

even the stone tiles bleed tears
Suddenly I want to wash away my sins
but realize my companions are

watching wondering why
I have fallen to my knees
why I too   am weeping

Dear Vincent, are the Trees in Saint Remy Truly so Maddening?

after The Starry Night by Vincent van Gogh

You could have painted the sky
using a branch of that tree,
broken and dipped it
in bright cobalt and gold
to swirl into the lovely,
lonely madness above.

You must have first danced that branch
across the sky, again and again
waltzing the hills, the night,
and then the clouds
into a miraculous turmoil

until, your curving path
left room only
for the punctuation of stars,
whirling in their own vortices.

Fireworks in your mind?

Or the repeating eye of a God
whom you want to ask
why *you* are the one
to be tortured in this place with
painting as your lone relief,

your one and only release
to disgorge
a burning brain
onto this churning canvas.

A Parting

after the painting Breezy by Jim Fish

When you left you didn't say good-bye
I didn't even hear your feet hit the floor
or the toilet flush
I woke to find your toothbrush gone

When I was washing my face
I felt more than sleep   wiped from my eyes
more than night sweat and sex go down
the drain in the shower

My heart seemed to shrink
felt as wrinkled and abandoned
as the old shirt you left
on the closet floor

You used to bring me butterflies
in books, the music of Botticelli,
and Band-aids for my blistered toes
I made you breakfast and brought

you to that Bodega Bay B&B
for bagels and star-fishing
in tidepools that reflected only
smiles of joy, eyes for each other

How sad that after all these months,
my only wave
was the one
your shirt gave me
when I left it out on the line

Master of Dark Looks

I had little sleep last night.
You never came to bed.
I am so tired of this.
My hand has worried
wrinkles in my face.

I'd like to ball fingers
into a fist or make them
into a claw to turn
on you instead of me.

Still, you peer over me as if I
am a naughty child to be punished.
Did I glance too long at the waiter?
At the man in the elevator?

Your scowling pout, practiced
nonchalance, may have worked
in the past, but you have
too often cultivated thorns
instead of roses.

Time for me to go.

Between Wolves and Stars

Though I try to capture in
a plaid wool blanket
the feeling of arms lost –
I am left with only
a pillow,
my own pale reflection,
the gooseflesh
of the glum and lonely.

I cannot duplicate
the blaze of bright eyes,
erupting low rumble of laughter,
cannot retrieve
what the ether has seized.
Grasping at ghosts,
sorrow engulfs me.

Maybe I'll join
the wolves in the woods,
howl at the waning moon.
I know you can't return my call
but it may help
to pretend my wolf sisters and I
are in harmony.
Pretend, I have friends
whose howls are also a lament
for your loss.

Then,
I would not be alone.
Then, perhaps
you'll hear, know

that I sing to the stars
because I miss
the gray-green sparkle
of your eyes.

When They're Too Young to Tell You Where it Hurts

Your stomach rumbled
like something between
an earthquake and a lion.
Then came the vomiting,
your rice pudding climbing
back up your throat
of its own volition.
You couldn't talk yet
so, you cried – your head
a burning red tomato,
fever 104.

At the ER,
the doctor made me put you
into an icy bath
to get down the high fever.
Knowing you wouldn't understand
why mommy was doing this,
I cringed and plunged you
into that frigid water
both of us wailing.
Your cloth diaper soaked up
the cold water, weighed you down
like an unabridged dictionary.

I struggled to keep you upright,
to keep your screaming lungs
from inhaling the bone-chilling water
until your temperature dropped,
until we were both
swaddled in towels on the floor
next to the tin wash tub.
One of us
still sobbing.

Revisiting a Loved One Lost
for David

First, you must try to forget the coffin.
Wipe away tears shed for what was,
what could have been.

Then, climb into his old green Peugeot.
Remember how you chuckled
that first night when he stopped
to call his parents.
He was 29.

Tiptoe up the parched, rickety, steps
into the farmhouse – plants standing,
hanging, coveting every surface.
Lie, tangled in the sheets, sweat.
Caress shoulders
even Atlas would envy.
Surround your face with
his long brown hair.
Listen to Joni Mitchell warble
while the tailless cat meows.

Then travel to Aspen
where he schusses down the slopes
"bend your knees, five dollars please" he says
joking with his young students.
Drink hot chocolate with Schnapps
while reading Lawrence Ferlinghetti
snuggled under a paisley duvet.

Stand in the vet's office in Spokane while
he sobs as the two of you put down
your Siberian Husky Saska
shot with a child's pellet gun

(who gives a child a pellet gun??)!
You both hold on and on but finally let go
of her black and white fur knowing you must both
finish studying for law school finals.

Fly into the Chugach Mountains of Alaska
where the waters of Cook Inlet sparkle,
reflect snow covered peaks, glass office towers
and the light lingers till well after midnight.

Find the small cabin by the zoo
with large, honey-colored logs
and the blond shaggy-haired boy
with a gap-toothed smile.

Try to focus on snow covered mountains,
moose that visit the yard
to munch whatever non-prickly bushes
abide, and each other.

There is plenty of him here
plenty of me
or there was for a while.

Don't ask me what
changed between us
I cannot tell you
where
you must go to find it.

Cannot not press rewind.
make myself
re-examine
that reel of film.

Diminishing

I can't explain
why the metal tarnished,
how the elation faded to
everyday ennui.

Living together,
we danced in and out
of each other's lives
for another year or two.

Things wanted in common...
Things wanted apart.

We continued to waltz
our Venn diagram into the rug –
middle shrinking like
a puddle after the storm.

Finally, we had to
acknowledge
that the knot, the bond
had come undone,
attempts to repair
miscarried.

Some things,
no amount
of sadness
or trying
can change.

4.
LETTING THE WAVES
WASH OVER ME

Snapshots from a Dream

We follow the nature trail
into the quiet. You think of
the great horned owl. Me of you.

Going through the mist
eyes seeking like torches,
things only the heart can find.

A view of sand swept dunes,
Moustaches of foam
floating on waves.

We laugh at the greedy seagull
stealing a French fry from a tourist
then dropping it into the bay.

The sand sticks to my toes,
tiny magnets of glass
warming sea-chilled phalanges.

A jellyfish with tenacles
too tender for stinging.

Sitting on a driftwood log,
salty hair stuck to my shoulders:
A mermaid without a tail.

Lying on a patchwork blanket,
the night wraps us
in her warm bodice

twirls us in
her skirt
of sequined stars.

Now You See Him, Now You Don't

There was an old lover in my mirror
when I brushed my teeth today.
He stepped out of the shower
still looking youthful, as in his forties.
He gave me a swat of his towel
and a sweet sloppy kiss.

When I opened my eyes post-kiss,
he was gone. I blinked again.
Wondered, if I'd spit him down the drain
with the toothpaste, or if he'd snuck out
to go to work, walk the dog?

I wanted to climb back into bed,
close my eyes, see if it was a dream.
If it was a dream, continue
to the place I hoped it would go.
Down byways of biceps
over to a hairy chest,
thin slick of sweat portending
moisture to come later, lower.

I tried to shake myself
back into today.
Not wanting to return,
I closed my eyes, sighed,
wondered
what tomorrow's
toothbrushing would bring.

Verklempt

It must come from the Dutch or German,
the word "verklempt" –
so harsh, dry.

Verklempt is how your throat feels,
when he tells you "It's over."

It's the tightening, the clamping,
the almost but not quite,
strangling sensation you get
when you can't swallow.

It's when tears have a mind of their own
creating puddles in the corners of your eyes,
and eventually your collar bone.

Where did it first come from?
It probably, once, was a medieval torture device –
something men feared,
and some wives wished for.

Or, it could have been a secret spell –
"Verklempt!" she said,
wand in outstretched hand.
Suddenly, he was silenced.

She smiled.
After all, turn about
is fair play.

Blank Page Syndrome (BPS)

Might white become my new favorite color?
It's the one I see the most, day after day,
lonely cursor winking at its glowing edge.

It's the color of snow, an egg (well some),
Italian marble, squishy marshmallows,
and luminous ghosts.

Perhaps, I should be happy to see a blank
page, free from the detritus of my mind.
No evidence of my internal struggle –

the glacial lack of movement
toward words being typed on a page
just to be deleted, juggled, cursed at.

Maybe, white
is the new black. So, for the moment

I'll savor these white-out conditions,
lose myself
in this eternal field of lint,
make a swirling tornado
of milky intent,
then lie down
until this chalky oblivion
takes me
to its heaven of alabaster
or hell
of ashen descent.

The Poetry Tree

When I was 15, the girl with glasses,
head always in a book,
my favorite haunt was an expansive old oak,
deep in my small southern woods –
a secret spot for seclusion.

After school, I'd climb into her limbs,
lie stretched across a sturdy gray branch,
strong enough to hold me – but lenient
enough to recoil gently in the wind.

We exchanged secrets.
I knew they were safe in her leafy embrace.
Who would she tell?
The brushy-tailed squirrel
who hopscotched through her branches?
The yellow moon
who came to call after I had gone?

No, there was a trust between us –
whispered by the wind, confirmed
by the coniferous pines surrounding us.
I distrusted only the Spanish moss
whose spiraled gray gnarls spoke of
questionable entanglements
and covert collaboration with chiggers.

Many days were spent stretched out in full
on the largest of the lower limbs,
letting the soft wind clear
the internal moss from my mind.

I'd seek that dreamlike state
that envelops prior to sleep,
the place poems are born –
perhaps meditation,
before I could name it.

Puppy Love

like a warm bowl
of puppy custard
he curls
and settles
nightly
into the small
of my back

he can't be petted
in that position
but seems happy
to simply share
the rhythm
of my breath

moving only during
my brief absences
to expand into a long
puppy log
stretching
and
usurping a little more
territory

until I return
and he softly
curls once more
into a warm vanilla
lumbar cushion

Willem

He arrived late for the party
almost an hour after his twin sister.

Rocky Marciano had nothing on him,
head bruised and swollen, yellow tinge
to his skin and he *was* a fighter.

Ahead were more battles but those
were punctuated by Escher-like
drawings and stories of comical

seagulls and crocodiles. Then later,
Japanese poems and Shakespearean insults.
He had a knack for humor, wordplay his forte.

Quiet around others, twin sister
his best friend – they had a bond so strong
Vince should have been selling it, a late-night infomercial.

Sweetest of all sous chefs and my cohort
in crime against crafts of every kind,
his reserved demeanor can mask his keen intellect.

Unafraid to fly to faraway lands,
explore other cultures, scale Mt. Fuji,
learn to scuba. He's an intrepid explorer

into realms musical and psychological,
as well as geographical. He gets lost
sometimes, but I'll always find him.

His creations, now digital,
with enchanting soundtracks
take you into playful fantasies

but still make those around him
smile the sweet smile of knowing:
Yes, that is definitely
"Willemesque."

Lemonade Dreams

On the patio
under the shade
of a red umbrella,
a ladybug finds
its way onto my arm.
I watch it meander
in its polka-dot jacket.

I have nowhere to go,
am happy to let my new friend
enjoy the stripe of sunlight
crossing my arm and
the blue and white
checked tablecloth
with the yellow pitcher.

Perhaps I'll put
my head next to hers,
let the lazy afternoon sun
lull me further
into ladybug
and lemonade
dreams.

5.

TREADING WATER

Mating Games

Two of a kind, a perfect pair,
many animals mate for life.

Famously, swans,
  some penguins,
      lovebirds,
          sandhill cranes.

Less well known, termites,
                    seahorses,
                            even the albatross.

Not mentioned: Humans – an unreliable species,

arms
        eternally reaching for connection but too often

they fall short,   *swerve,*
                    are af*ra*id,
too PROUD,

                        too ti_r_
                            e̲
                                d̲.
              We circle in and OUT

  swoopclose, then   waltz wi de

            over skies
        between continents
          across the street

until

we are
worlds

a   p   a   r   t.

Glitter

My first reaction was to cover my face
as I felt the prickly glitter
landing there in showers
One-two-three
and I blinked awake
to see your 3-year-old smile,
chubby glitter-covered fingers
working above me.

"GRRR.... you woke the tickle monster!"
I started crawling after you
across the thick knobby carpet, shaking my head,
shedding colorful glitter from my face.
You ran giggling into the kitchen –
there was shelter between Mommy's
soft black leggings and Truffles'
furry wiggling body.

Oh.... No.... not awake
and the glitter-box is no more.
No more Joni in the kitchen.
No more Truffles bounding to the door.
No more smiles, wiggles, giggles.
It was just the tapping of
rain on the skylight
that woke me.

Road Tripping

Riding thru the Oregon hills
Winding this way and that
the towering hillside stones
with only a few trees take on shapes:
Face parts of the Greek gods.

A smooth cheek here, a wrinkled
forehead there, a slanted nose,
and what could be full lips.
I laugh when even the moss
plays its part as nose hair and when,
after dozing a bit,

I glance out at a
scrubby winter hillock and
a copse of green-gray bushes
immediately strike me
as Zeus's pubic hair.

Okay, I ask my partner,
how far to the coffee shop?
Motel?

The Doors With No Numbers

Corridors long, doors without numbers.
How to find my exam room?
Walking endlessly, then
at a desk, blue book ready
but no pen or pencil.
Everyone else is writing
The timer has started,
I can't interrupt.

Then I'm writing
and writing for what seems like hours.
But when I peek back –
my work vanishes.
I watch the words I've written
fly into the air,
dissolve into the ether.

I want to banish all tests
from my dream-dance-card,
remove them from my menu.

Next time I'm running
by rooms with no numbers,
I'll keep on walking.
Play hooky from class.
Look for the first exit.
Pull the fire alarm.
Flunk the exam.

After all, what can they do now?
Revoke my AARP card?

Nose Job

I was the serious big sister,
there for support. You
smiling (you were always
smiling) – unworried, being prepped.

The wait while you were under
dragged on…
I stared at the wallpaper,
tongue depressor beige.
Paged through many magazines
from the waiting room

but kept wondering – did you really
need a rhinoplasty?
Yes, your nose was a little
crooked, not unlike mine.

When you came back, you were
not smiling. Bandages cocooned
your face. There was purple and
black swelling where your eyes

had been. The room seemed hot,
the walls now melting. Nausea
like morning sickness swept me.
I wasn't pregnant.

Then I was on the floor.
Later I drove you home.
You slept sitting up on the couch.
Your head a thundercloud –

dark shadows with occasional
showers, or rather, leakage.
I slept on the floor beside you
suppressing my own storm.

White Buffalo

Did you ever see a glacier calve? It starts with a low rumble – stomach growl to earthquake. Then growing louder, the glacier moves in slow-motion until the noise reaches a roar, the belly starts to crack, like thunder! You expect to see lightening streak the sky. A gargantuan chunk of ice, the white calf, an iceberg, slides into the sea. Around it, white foam churns into a broad wave – steaming like a booming waterfall. Sometimes, it's not just a single calf – the whole face of the glacier melts, calving multiples. A thundering herd of frosty buffalo stampeding into warmer water beneath. Will these glaciers suffer the same fate as the buffalo? Rolling water displaced by felled calves seems to dwarf your boat, a tsunami several stories tall: Wrath of the White Buffalo the indigenous peoples might say. You release a deep breath as the wave dissipates. You think you're safe, but sea-level continues to rise as each glacier melts.

> *White buffalo grazed quietly*
> *for centuries. Like ghosts,*
> *not all creatures rest peacefully.*

A Letter to Franz Kafka

The world will freely offer itself
to you to be unmasked. It has no choice,
it will roll in ecstasy at your feet.   *Franz Kafka*

Dear Mr. Kafka,

Oh, that it was so…
but I fear today,
our world is playing
hide and seek.

It is immune to our charms
whirls in the solar system
playing games with Venus and Mars.
It is tired of being host

to parasitic humans who take,
but give little in return.
Our invitation to the party may soon
be revoked, our shelf-life expiring
before the sell-by date.

We do not play well
with other species. We hunt
them to extinction.
turn the communal air yellow,
lungs black, rain poison,
then reject responsibility.

We cannot even agree among ourselves.
Our waste is legend. Our moon fears
becoming a dumping ground.
Our sun would like to shade *his* view
Can you not feel his wrath
in droughts and in fires?

Before too long Mr. Kafka,
the world may only
be home
to cockroaches.

War

like a croc in a muddy river
ugly and terrible
it rears its hateful head

not even a few years pass
not even one year, or season
before it starts again somewhere
before some daughter or son

father or mother
in some country
far or near must
strap on a weapon

march to the diatribe
of some dictator or
oligarch's unbridled greed

the innocent must bare their teeth
the croc needs red meat

Dental Hygiene

I close my eyes because it's better that way.
The light is bright above, and
I know the drill, so to speak.

The hygienist is giving me instructions
which I understand, although they sound
like the parents do in Peanuts cartoons.

She starts by measuring my gum recession –
Calling out numbers to a colleague: 3-2, 3-3, 2-2
while piercing my gums with a pointy crooked wire.

At least that's what's on the end of the instrument
I can see if I open my eyes.
She says my numbers have improved,

but I find my hands, clasped together in my lap,
still unnaturally gripping each other – as if
by some magnetic force, even as I'm trying to relax.

She asks if I'm okay with "the ultrasonic."
"Sure," I say, not sure I know what
that means. Then the sound brings it back.

There is a high-pitched squeaking-squealing
behind high-pressure noise. It sounds like a wee mouse
is being tortured with a water cannon. Repeatedly.

Once that is done, we move on to scaling.
I picture a tiny mountain climber on my teeth.
The reality is a scraping sensation, a garden gnome abrading stones.

I try not to think about it that way. Instead
I think about fish being scaled on a stainless
steel sink. Somehow, that doesn't help.

Then I'm ready for a polish and I breathe
a sigh of relief, knowing this is the final stretch.
The hygienist sends me home with fluoride rinse

and instructions to return in six months.
I'm already dreading it, so I swear to start
flossing – regularly. And I mean it.

Crow Wisdom

Crow
older than
the felled tree
where it sits
each morning

ponders days
when slender fish
were plentiful

misses
the old man
who used to walk
the log

can almost see
his reflection
if the lake is still
and the clouds
linger low

Old friends
don't depart
they sometimes
stop by
in the shadows

Death Throes

for Roy E. Gabbert, Sr. and his children

I. The Cancer Was a Beast

First in the prostate
it feasted on and off for almost 20 years
before starting its extended journey
into other body parts.
Toward the end, it gnawed away
at his spine, dissolving it
into a gelatinous mass.

Daddy being Daddy,
thought it was just a matter of –
the right doctors
the right research
the right clinical studies.
He attended medical seminars.
The doctors knew him by name.
He flew to Cleveland and Texas, other clinics.

Finally, it came down to
the sheer brutality of Cancer and Chemo vs. Roy E. Gabbert.
If the drugs were a one-two punch –
he was on the ropes, down for the count.
Who knows what the cancer felt,
but it did not seem fazed.

He couldn't eat, could barely drink.
The sores camped out on his tongue –
ulcers on holiday, squatters with
no intention of moving on
at the end of the month.

II. "The Buzzards Are Circling"

Three thousand miles away in Alaska
I heard it all second-hand:
No, he didn't want visitors
My sister went anyway.
No one could keep her
from her Daddy.
Daddy's sister, Aunt Ann, came too.

He said, "I see
the buzzards are circling."

We were always alike, Me and Dad.
I understood wanting
to be alone with your pain.
But finally, I wanted to see him anyway –
one last time.

My sister insisted on a repeat performance.
We were in the airport in Minneapolis
waiting for our flight to Cincy when
My brother called and said,
"He's gone."

Still five hours to get there –
first flying, then speeding
through rural Ohio. The
University of Cincinnati
was waiting for the body
he'd donated to science.

III. At the Morgue

We went to a kind of morgue,
not a hospital or funeral home.
He was laid out on a cold stone table
smaller than he ever seemed in life.
The paperwork said 5'9" – so short
and so pale in his cornflower blue
hospital gown. Where were his glasses?
He didn't need them now,
but seemed so naked without them.

I kissed him on the cheek
touched his hand, closed my eyes.
Then… my sister
began her production number.

Cassette tape with music.
I don't remember now what.
A letter from my Mom,
she insisted on reading aloud.
The staff seemed confused,
our younger brother and
sister very tolerant.

Then they took him away,
like a waiter whisking away your meal
before you'd finished eating.

Later that evening at home
the lights flickered – my sister was sure
Daddy was giving us a sign.

By then I was sure the sign read:
Leave me in peace.

IV. Aftermath

There were articles in the local papers:
"Longtime Adams County Lawyer Dead of Cancer"
Roy Junior will continue the practice.

No mention of a funeral.
The current Missus didn't want one.
But people came to the door for days
bringing food and flowers.

An elderly black woman said
he was the only one who would
represent her back in the 1950s.
She'd paid him with a live chicken.

We stayed a few days longer
playing board games and
eating too much pimento cheese
spread from the IGA.

My brother's laugh was hardy
and unrestrained, contagious
just like Daddy's.
My baby sister, a storyteller,
and shy like me –
Both an unexpected joy.
We vowed to keep in touch
but haven't, not really.

Is it easier to just slip back
into the patterns set up for us
all those decades ago by the "adults"
as if we're still children
who must follow tired rules
which now have no teeth?

Is it too late for us kids
now in our own senescence,
growing old,
to do the hard work of
being a real family?

Morphine Dreams

Spiders turn into crabs
attack birds from their webs.
Baby without a bassinet
sleeps perched on a bare ledge.

I've fallen in the river
floating downward still asleep.
Somehow, I haven't drowned yet
blowing kisses to the fish.

Koi swim in sewage water,
orange feet walk onto shore.
Cottage made of honeycomb,
a large bee at the door.

Flowers in tower tall vases,
dead/decapitated heads.
Somehow, I haven't drowned yet.
I'm covered all in red.

Afraid to leave my bed.

Even dreams are threatened
I fear to rest my head
you may think this is all nonsense
silly babbling, nothing more

but can you tell me why then
the gestapo's at my door?

Acknowledgements

Finally, my sincere thanks to the editors of the publishers below who previously published my poems, sometimes in earlier versions:

Invisible, *"How We Change,"* San Francisco Writers Foundation Writing Contest Anthology (Poetry Finalist 2024) January 2025

Kisses, accepted for publication, *Just So,* Redwood Writers 2025 Poetry Anthology

Baby Girl of My Heart, Schuylkill Valley Journal, Volume 60, June 2025

Bloodlines, accepted for publication, Bay to Ocean Journal, 2025

Thunder, "SCARS: A Beyond Words Anthology," a Beyond Words publication, May 2025

Childbirth, 1950s Rural Ohio, "The Weight of Motherhood," Moonstone Press Anthology 2023

Posthumous Epithalamion, Delta Poetry Review, Volume: 6, Issue: 16, *for Ethel and Sid,* Winter 2024

PaPaw, "Phases," Redwood Writers 2023 Poetry Anthology

Reckoning, "Ekphrastic Poetry," Moonstone Press Anthology 2023

We Gather at the Altar, "Wings of Stars," Blue Light Press Anthology 2024

Tangled, "Wings of Stars," Blue Light Press Anthology 2024

A Parting, "Wings of Stars," Blue Light Press Anthology 2024

Now You See Him, Now You Don't, "Wings of Stars," Blue Light Press Anthology 2024

Splitting Hairs, "Beyond Distance," Redwood Writers 2021 Poetry Anthology

On the Edge, Vision and Verse, California Writers Club Ekphrastic Anthology 2024

The Poetry Tree, Poetry Breakfast, online poetry magazine at PoetryBreakfast.com, October 16, 2023

It's Happening Again, Climate Shift, North Bay Poetics Anthology 2023

Blank Page Syndrome, Crossroads, Redwood Writers 2022 Poetry Anthology

Puppy Love, Love Is, Love Poems Vol. II, Edited by Johnny M. Tucker, Jr. 2022

White Buffalo, Climate Shift, North Bay Poetics Anthology 2023

Glitter, "Phases," Redwood Writers 2023 Poetry Anthology

Dear Mr. Kafka "Poured Out from the Big Dipper," Blue Light Press Anthology, 2023

Doors with No Numbers, "Poured Out from the Big Dipper," Blue Light Press Anthology, 2023

Dental Hygiene, "Crossroads," Redwood Writers 2022 Poetry Anthology

Crow Wisdom, accepted for publication, *Just So,* Redwood Writers 2025 Poetry Anthology

About the Author

Robin Gabbert has poems in state, national, and international poetry anthologies. She is the 2025 winner of the Fran Claggett-Holland award for her contributions to poetry and the poetry community. Her poem *Invisible* was a finalist in the 2024 San Francisco Writers Conference Contest for Poetry and she was long-listed for the Frontier Poetry *"(Not) In Love"* Tanka Challenge in 2024. Her chapbook of ekphrastic poetry and art – *The Clandestine Life of Paintings, in Poems* was published in 2022 and *Diary of a Mad Poet* 2020. Robin's passion is to "capture the essence" of a situation or feeling in a few well-chosen words. She teaches, and is a frequent speaker on ekphrastic poetry, and is a poetry judge and editor for the California Writers Club and North Bay Poetics. When not writing, she likes to frolic with her pup Hamish, spend time with family, and read mysteries. See more about her at www.robingabbert.com.

www.ingramcontent.com/pod-product-compliance
Lightning Source LLC
Chambersburg PA
CBHW022202080426
42734CB00006B/547